bring | teach | keep

ILLUMINATING THE BIBLICAL MODEL OF EVANGELISM

Chuck Anderson & John Furness

bringteachkeep.com

Table of Contents

Preface

Do you get a "punched-in-the-gut" feeling every time you hear the word evangelism? If so, you're certainly not alone. For years, many in the Lord's church have been taught a narrow view of evangelism in which all members are called to be teachers of the gospel, and that has frightened much of the body into idleness. Yet, we read just the opposite in the pages of the Bible. Instead, we're told that few should assume the responsibility to teach (James 3:1). What have we been missing?

It's imperative that we gain a deeper understanding of the three distinct areas that comprise the biblical model of evangelism—bringing, teaching and keeping. All three roles are essential to the long term success of any evangelistic effort. By telling all that they must teach, we prevent many from developing and nurturing their true talents. Each Christian must discover the area (or areas) in which God has gifted them. This book was written to help you come to an understanding of where you fit into the grand scheme of evangelism.

I pray that this material will help you find your God-given role in the biblical model of evangelism. Study the chapters over and over, add your insights to ours, join the body in service where you properly fit, and prepare yourself for sustained congregational growth.

~ Chuck Anderson

Introduction

You picked up this book and made it past the title page, so I'm led to believe that you have an interest in evangelism. Maybe you want to share the gospel with others but don't know how to start. Or perhaps you're currently active in evangelism but want to become more effective. Either way, a healthy desire to serve the Lord is quite noteworthy. You see, these days many Christians don't think they're cut out for evangelism.

Since the beginning of time, Satan has used his influence to deceive mankind, and he continues to do so by making Christians fearful of evangelism. The father of lies has convinced us that leading lost souls to Jesus requires either a Ph.D. in theology or many years of experience as a pulpit minister. He has made us believe that all Christians must train to be teachers and lead Bible studies. It's my goal in this book to prove to you instead that God has blessed every Christian with a unique and important role in evangelism.

Ephesians 4:15-16 is commonly referenced in sermons and studies, and many of you are probably familiar with the passage. I want to share it with you again and ask you to think about it as it relates to evangelism: "Rather, speaking the truth in love, we are to grow up in every way into Him who is the head, into Christ, from whom the whole body, joined and held together by every joint with which it is equipped, when each part is working properly, makes the body grow so that it builds itself up in love" (Ephesians 4:15-16).

Do you find it interesting how readily we Christians relate the metaphor of the body to tasks within the church like communion preparation, nursery duty, and lawn maintenance? Yet, when referring to evangelism, we call all members to teach instead of asking each person to locate and utilize his or her own unique gift. We must listen to the voice of God when He says, "be not many of you teachers" (James 3:1).

Paul asked for his thorn in the flesh to be removed three times and God said, "My grace is sufficient for you, for My power is made great in weakness" (2 Corinthians 12:7-9). You may consider yourself weak and invaluable in evangelism, but perhaps you've just been forced into an inappropriate role. When you find your proper place in the God-designed and God-ordained model of evangelism, He will bless your efforts to influence the hearts of seeking men and women.

I present this book to you with hope that it will help you unlock your evangelistic gift and find where your God-given role in evangelism lies. It is not an exhaustive work, but a framework for self-discovery and talent utilization.

Prayerfully ask for His guidance as you mature and build upon it, understanding that it is His power and influence that ultimately wins souls.

HOW THIS MATERIAL CAME TO BE

One of the first decisions I made as a new Christian was to tell my friends and family about Jesus. I was so excited about my newfound salvation and thought that they would turn to the Savior without hesitation, in spite of the fact that I had no idea what the scriptures taught about evangelizing the lost. Completely inexperienced, I picked up my "Bible-shaped sledge hammer" and went on the attack, condemning the religious practices of everybody I knew. My evangelistic fervor was poorly channeled, and it pushed people away instead of drawing them to Jesus.

The barrage continued for a few years until my father-in-law sat me down one day and frankly asked, "So, how is that working out for you? Have you led anyone to Christ with that kind of approach?" I didn't understand that I was acting like a bull in a china shop, smashing and shattering the interest of my friends and family instead of building them up in love. Seeing the ineffectiveness of my efforts, I knew there had to be a better way.

Years later, I saw a timeline presentation that placed the events of the Bible in chronological order. It showed how everything from the dawn of creation points to Jesus. This made a lot of sense to me. It organized what knowledge I had into a spiritual filing cabinet of sorts, which made the redemption story so much clearer. I spent years testing and reshaping the method and (with the help of many) modeled it into a presentation designed to quickly lead the lost to the Savior by conveying to them the completeness and cohesiveness of the biblical narrative.

The timeline was a hit! I taught and baptized many very receptive students. Yet, despite its success in bringing people to the Savior, converts seemed to fall away after a short period of time. We were bringing and teaching the lost, so what was missing? I found the answer upon closer inspection of the second chapter of Acts. "And all who believed were together and had all things in common. And they were selling their possessions and belongings and distributing the proceeds to all, as any had need. And day by day, attending the temple together and breaking bread in their homes, they received their food with glad and generous hearts..." (Acts 2:44-46).

Peter's sermon moved 3,000 souls to the waters of baptism that day, yet I had never taken the time to think about the implications of such a mass conversion. Who cared for the spiritual needs of so many newborn babes? It was then that I realized the importance of the Christian support system. New Christians must receive personal attention from mature brethren and regularly socialize with the saints to stay focused and safe.

From that point on, I began to emphasize the role of the brother's keeper whenever one of my students became a Christian, and the attrition rate dropped dramatically. Their spiritual growth and increasing Bible knowledge became evident in their everyday walk. The example of the early church showed me that we must not only bring and teach the lost, but that we must also work diligently and intentionally as a community to keep them faithful for life.

FOOD *for* THOUGHT

The biblical model of evangelism is so successful because it was designed by the Lord Himself. During the past few years, 35 students have become Christians after hearing the timeline presentation. Of those 35 people, a whopping 29 are still faithful because of an active brother's keeper ministry in our congregation. Brethren, that's off the charts. As you read on, I hope you'll see the wisdom in these methods because they are wholly Bible-derived.

UNDERSTANDING THIS MATERIAL

It is critical that this material be understood in the context of evangelism. When I speak about teaching the lost in this book, I'm specifically referring to the act of opening up the Bible and leading somebody to an understanding of what they must do to be saved. I do not deny the power of letting our light so shine before others that they see our good works and give glory to God (Matthew 5:16). Our example is tremendously important. However, I believe that only the Word can teach people how to be in a right relationship with the Lord.

I've heard it said that all are teachers because "anyone can tell their story." Undoubtedly, telling your story can be an effective tool to help you reach out to those who may share a similar experience or thought. But make no mistake—neither my story nor your story can save one soul. The only story with saving power is that of Jesus Christ. Consider the woman at the well, who went back into town to share her divine encounter. Did her story directly convert anybody? Of course, the answer is no. But it did pique their curiosity enough to bring them out to the one who could teach them further. The people of the town believed not because of what she said, but because they "heard him themselves" (John 4:42).

When I speak about being a brother's keeper in this book, I am focusing on the new Christian. Certainly, it is important for mature brethren to keep an eye out for one another, but they must always remember that the babe in Christ is most vulnerable to Satan's schemes. To watch out for them is a pressing matter.

Guilt is a terrible motivator in a volunteer army.
This book is designed to explore the evangelistic thought

process, so it may inspire thoughts of guilt. Always remember that Jesus did not save us to live a life of guilt. We need to treat guilt like we do a headache—find out why it exists and apply an appropriate remedy. Evangelism should be motivated by a deep desire to bring lost souls to Jesus. No one deserves His grace, but He's given it anyway. Talk about spring in your step!

A skilled person was a novice at one time.

Becoming effective in evangelism requires time, so don't expect immediate success. Understand that evangelism is a way of life and not relegated to specific "work days." It is a continual growth process. Don't be too hard on yourself as you encounter obstacles along the way. Learn from the stories I've included about my own mistakes and ways to avoid them. The bumps and bruises are all worth it for the eternal joy that He promises to those who love Him and obey His commands.

Balance is crucial.

We cannot abandon our families in order to knock doors, attend seminars and study evangelism all day, nor can we become so engrossed in the cares and pleasures of the world that evangelism has no place in our lives. It's imperative that you find your place in evangelism and slowly incorporate it into your life. With consistency, it will effortlessly weave itself into the fabric of who you are.

A Necessary Mental Adjustment

When speaking at evangelism seminars, I begin by asking the group where they feel their importance in evangelism lies. Usually, my question is met by a lengthy silence. I then ask the audience to complete the following sentence:

"I feel valuable, useful and important in my congregation's evangelism efforts because I _____."

Before proceeding, answer this question yourself. If you are like most seminar attendees, you also paused to search for an honest answer. Generally, I receive one of three responses, which I've included below with my straightforward assessment of each (I do not mean to be unnecessarily brash, but this is a serious subject).

Response 1: "I don't do enough."

How much is too little or too much? We all need to be involved in evangelism in some capacity, but must be careful not to lean toward a works-based salvation for justification. It isn't about volume, but rather blooming where you're planted.

Response 2: "I can't handle the rejection."
The truth of the matter is that you will be rejected—either by man or by God. It's your choice (Mt. 10:32-33).

Response 3: "I don't have all the answers."
Who has all the answers but the Lord Himself? Always point to the Savior and go to the Word to find the answers to difficult questions.

Jesus said that He is "sending us out as sheep among wolves, so be wise as serpents yet gentle as doves" (Matthew. 10:16). The example He uses is so colorfully graphic. Can you imagine throwing a ewe into a pack of wolves and expecting it to survive without some sort of intervention? Evangelism is not a simple, "lay-down and let it happen" sort of mission. It can take great time and effort, and has its own set of challenges. Always remember that Jesus has promised not to leave your side so long as you are faithful and obedient to Him. God will provide wisdom to overcome the obstacles that Satan constructs if we ask Him in prayer (James 1:5). There are so many seeking souls in the world. We need to become wiser at finding them and leading them to the Savior.

In the coming sections, we'll investigate the biblical model of evangelism to show how each person fits into God's grand scheme for saving souls. Along the way, I want to share a story about a young man named Brock, who has a heart for lost souls but a very misguided approach.

BROCK'S DILEMMA

Brock has been a Christian for some time and is tired of the stomach ache he gets every time someone mentions evangelism. He is fed up with hiding behind his excuses and fears, and decides that this week he will speak to someone about their soul. Tuesday evening, Brock looks outside to find his neighbor John in his own backyard, admiring his freshly cut lawn. He walks out the back door over to the fence and, after some small talk, engages John in the following dialogue:

Brock: "Hey John. I was wondering if you and your family worship anywhere on Sundays?"

John: "Sure do. We're members at the large church right down the street."

Brock: "That's great. So, you believe baptism is necessary for salvation, right?"

John: "Oh, absolutely..."

Brock feels great about John's answer, but doesn't realize that he has set up a figurative bear trap and is beginning to quickly walk toward it.

John: "...that's why I'm so happy my parents took care of that before I was even 2 months old when I was sprinkled by the priest."

Brock meanders toward the bear trap, caught off guard by John's elaboration.

Brock: "John, the Bible says that baptism is a complete burial in water. An adult believer must be totally immersed for it to be scriptural."

John: "Well, I know your church does it that way, but we sprinkle in our church. I've even seen drawings of Jesus standing waist deep in water with John the Baptist pouring water over His head. Burying, sprinkling or pouring ... it's all the same."

The trap is now just a step or two away.

Brock: "John, it's not the same! The Greek word for baptism is baptizo, and it means a total immersion in water. This is what the Bible teaches and those other ways are unacceptable to God."

CLANG! The trap snaps around Brock's leg.

John: "Brock, I appreciate you as a neighbor, so from now on let's not discuss religion until we get to Heaven together, each on our own path."

Brock builds a wall between himself and John when he could have built a bridge. Unwilling to quit, he tries the same approach with family and coworkers on a number of topics—instrumental music in the worship service, the frequency of communion, and the proper day of worship. As he continues to build walls, Satan convinces him that evangelism just isn't something that God has blessed him to be involved in. Brock nestles into his pew, content to be involved with anything but evangelism.

ANALYZING BROCK'S EFFORTS

In your mind, did Brock follow the wisdom of Jesus and the inspired apostles when he reached out to John? I see three glaring issues with Brock's approach that should be addressed immediately.

1. **Where was Jesus in the conversation?**
    People need to be converted to Jesus, not to the different rites of the church. If someone is fully committed to Christ, there should be no issue with standards of worship. Everything will fall into place. Perhaps, Brock should have brought up the name of Jesus to see where John was at in his spiritual walk.

2. **Was John seeking?**
    Matthew 6:33 says "But seek first the kingdom of God and his righteousness, and all these things will be add-

ed to you." From this, we can infer that only true seekers will find the truth. Many times, we need to plant the "need to seek thought" long before teaching can begin. Brock could have asked John what his thoughts were about Jesus, the Bible or the church, using questions that would lead John to think about his stance (i.e. "What are you doing to search for God" or "What ministries are you involved in that help you draw closer to God"). John's answers would have given Brock good insight into whether he was really seeking or not. The questions could have also prompted John to consider his position and think about seeking at a later date.

3. Was the approach appropriate?

Brock's intentions were pure, but he attacked John's faith and worship, which led to a debate instead of a study. How do you feel when you're harshly criticized for your convictions? Do you tend to receive the counsel of your accuser or shut down and withdraw like John did? Brock could have better used this opportunity to invite John to study the Bible instead of pulling doctrine out of the air in an attempt to "correct" John's beliefs.

Is the attack/debate approach effective?

No one likes to hear "you're wrong!" It is critical to understand that while our mission from Jesus is to go and teach, we can only teach willing listeners. Brock's approach did not foster a willingness in John to learn more. An "over the fence" conversation can be a great way to openly discuss religious matters or to see if someone is seeking, but is only effective when the hearer is ready to receive the Word. Brock, ready to put his energized spirit into motion, failed to consider whether John was seeking (Matthew 7:7).

Since John was not seeking in this scenario, it would have done Brock well to ask John what he likes about the church he attends and just listen to him. This is great information to have for future conversations with John.

A prophet is not without honor except in his hometown.

Brock may not have been the best person to share the gospel with John because of their established relationship. In Matthew 13:53-58, Jesus taught many things that astonished His listeners, but since they all knew Him as "the carpenter's son," it was hard for them to receive His words. I am certainly not saying that we should keep the good news of Jesus from our friends and family, but there may be a way to share it in which they're more likely to listen. Perhaps someone in Brock's congregation could have taken the lead on trying to teach John.

Are we all teachers?

In our scenario, it is clear that Brock had not developed as a teacher of the gospel. In fact, he may not have had that gift at all. He had great enthusiasm, but at that point was a round peg in a square hole—zealous without wisdom/

knowledge and possessing a wonderful spirit soon to be discouraged into idleness.

James 3:1 says, "Be not many of you teachers" and Ephesians 4:11 says that He put some in the church as pastors and teachers. We mistakenly convey the wrong message when we state that all need to teach the lost directly. It is our job as Christians to see that the lost are taught, whether we bring, teach or keep.

A total life change in one study?

Should Brock have expected John to completely abandon all of his beliefs and convert after one conversation? I do not think it is realistic to expect to convert somebody after one study or conversation, especially with no idea of what they believe, where they are in life, or whether they are truly seeking.

In Luke 14:28, Jesus suggests that the wise count the cost before building a tower or going to war. Becoming a Christian is a decision that should require much thought and introspection. If one does not forsake all for Him he cannot be His disciple (verse 33).

We need to make sure that lost souls are converted to Jesus, not to baptism or any other church doctrine. My experience has taught me that while it is possible to immerse someone after one study, their faithfulness is typically short lived. We're often so eager to get them into the water that we avoid telling them anything that may make them wait. Remember, if a person is truly seeking, God will grant the increase in His own time. He never fails!

FOOD *for* THOUGHT

"Now you are the body of Christ and individually members of it ... Are all apostles? Are all prophets? Are all teachers? Do all work miracles? Do all possess gifts of healing? Do all speak with tongues? Do all interpret? But earnestly desire the higher gifts." (1 Corinthians 12:27, 29-31)

BROCK'S WELL INTENDED EFFORT

Most of the people I've told this story to admit that, just like Brock, we often share the gospel in a way that overlooks God's wisdom. We so often follow our own intuition and understanding, which ultimately leads to failure.

In the previous sections, we examined three major issues with Brock's attempt. You may see more holes in his approach, and I encourage you to make note of those. I believe it is our responsibility to do everything possible to keep souls from hell. Use the following question as a mental guide: **How can I make the environment as rich as possible for the lost soul to understand and obey the Truth?** If we can do this to the best of our ability, then we can know that our efforts were a success in God's eyes.

I hope that Brock's story has not discouraged you, but has instead made you curious to discover more about the complete biblical model of evangelism. As we go into more detail, you will learn to identify your gift and see where you fit into God's plan for evangelism. Keep your chin up—exciting solutions lie ahead!

Unlocking Your Evangelistic Gift

Let's start the discovery process by temporarily removing the many deep-seated beliefs we have about evangelism, and get right down to the very core. Evangelism is about bringing lost souls into contact with Jesus, teaching them of the obedience He requires, and keeping them safe in Christ for life. There are three major roles in the biblical model of evangelism:

1. **"Bringers"** (John 1:40-46, Acts 10:24)
2. **"Teachers"** (Matthew 28:18-20)
3. **"Brother's keepers"** (Acts 2:44-47, 1 Thess.1-2)

Each one of these areas is a training ground all its own, yet all three must be in place for evangelism to succeed. Think about it. If we don't bring, who will we teach? If we bring, but don't teach, there's no one to keep. If we bring and teach, but don't keep, we all lose. Not only is there no gain, but a soul is worse off (2 Peter 2:20-22).

Knowing that each of these areas is of equal importance in the grand scheme of evangelism, I feel that the role of the brother's keeper is most pressing at this time in the life of the Lord's church. We so often reach out into the community to seek lost souls, but forget to ask, "What will we do when they actually come?"

When building a house, a knowledgeable carpenter does not start with the roof. First, a foundation is set. Next, walls are erected. Finally, the roof is fitted on top of the structure. When the house is complete, we value it as a whole, realizing the importance of each component. The system of evangelism functions the same way, and a strong brother's keeper program is the needed foundation for any congregation. Let me show you how bringing and teaching suffer without such an effort in place.

THE CHURCH WITHOUT KEEPERS

When Andrew brought his brother Peter to Jesus (John 1:35-42), the Savior readily received Peter with patience, instruction, love and direction—the spiritual food necessary for strong, sustained growth. He knew that Peter would need to grow in wisdom, in stature, and in favor with God and man, just as He had from childhood (Luke 2:52). In fact, all new Christians must be nurtured in these four areas to become strong in the faith.

Unfortunately, most congregations confess that they have no system in place to actively keep their members faithful. I see this much like a bucket with a hole in the bottom, into which water is being steadily poured. To keep the bucket full, we should not increase the rate at which the water enters the bucket, but rather plug the hole in the bottom as quickly as possible. I am not suggesting that we ever stop bringing and teaching lost souls, but we must be prepared to address the new Christian's issues first and foremost, plugging the figurative "hole" in our evangelistic system.

1. The Pipe (Bringers)
Christians who bring a steady stream of lost souls to be taught.

2. The Tap (Teachers)
Those who instruct and lead souls to the truth of the gospel.

3. The Stream (New Christians)
Those who respond to the gospel and are added to the church.

4. The Bucket (Your Congregation)
The members of your local flock who serve together.

5. The Hole
There's something missing in the evangelism process...

6. The Leakage (Those who fall away)
Christians who return to the world after being added to the church.

7. The Cork (Brother's Keepers)
Those who work diligently to provide for the New Christians' spiritual, physical, intellectual, and social needs (Luke 2:52).

We must meet their...
PHYSICAL NEEDS

Just as the new Christians in Acts 2 shared with one another, so should we be ready to meet the physical needs of our new family, if they are struggling.

We must meet their...
NEED FOR WISDOM

Wisdom comes from maturity, so we cannot expect babes to possess as much as the mature. Instead, we must show them, through the Word, how to live wisely.

CORK

Lk. 2:52

We must meet their...
SOCIAL NEEDS

We are all called to be different than the world, and that can be tough for a new Christian. They may need to leave their old friends and we need to fill the void.

We must meet their...
SPIRITUAL NEEDS

New Christians are easy prey for Satan. He will come after them immediately, and we must ensure that the new Chrisitan is being fed the pure milk of the Word.

The Brother's Keeper

The Scriptures teach very clearly that few will be saved. In Luke 13:24, Jesus exhorts us to "strive to enter through the narrow gate, for many... will seek to enter and will not be able." It's humbling to think that only 8 were saved in the days of Noah, only 3 were saved from the destruction of Sodom and Gomorrah, and only 2 of the 603,550 men aged 20 or older were delivered into the promised land of Canaan. Throughout the ages, God is ruler of a remnant.

Knowing that few will put on Christ in this life, why do you suppose that we spend so little effort securing new Christians? I believe this is the result of another of Satan's masterfully crafted lies. He wants us to believe that once a person becomes a Christian they are safe for life, completely invulnerable. He focuses us time and time again on the pursuit of the "Next One," while in the meantime we completely neglect the needs of the "New One."

I tend to think of the Brother's Keeper as the "forgotten" facet of our evangelistic efforts because most congregations fail to recognize its necessity to the growth and sustenance of the flock. An active Brother's Keeper ministry serves a number of crucial purposes:

- It secures new Christians by providing the 4 necessary areas of growth: physical, spiritual, social, wisdom (Luke 2:52).
- It provides new Christians with instruction on how to appropriately approach friends and family without running them off.
- It gives mature Christians the chance to minister to new souls.
- It extends the network of contacts, to which the church can reach out and teach.
- It establishes a foundation for a congregation to sustain growth and potentially plant another congregation.
- Most importantly, it completes the New Testament model of evangelism by putting people to work using the God-given gifts they possess.

A BROTHER NEEDING TO BE KEPT

The year I became a Christian, I met my future wife Michelle. She was a strong Christian woman who had been raised in the church, and I loved spending time with her and her family. That Thanksgiving, they involved me in many of their Christmas traditions—decorating the house, tree-trimming, cookie baking, and present wrapping. I had just converted from Catholicism, so Christmas festivities had been a part of my life from childhood. In fact, I actually thought that Michelle's family played the holiday down a bit. There was no advent celebration, Christmas pageant, or midnight mass. It certainly wasn't the excess I was used to seeing, but pleasant nonetheless, so I redefined my concept of Christmas to fit with theirs. Surely, I thought, Michelle's family would know how to celebrate such an important holiday properly. Little did I know that Satan was using the opportunity to set and bait a trap for me.

Just before the holiday, I had a chance encounter with one of my new Christian brothers. We talked some about our Christmas plans, and then, out of nowhere, he produced a tract from his pocket. On the front of the small pamphlet, in a bold and authoritative typeface, was the title *Why Christians Shouldn't Celebrate Christmas*. I was instantly taken aback. Michelle's family seemed to think Christmas was okay, and they were certainly rooted in the faith. Befuddled, I sought guidance from another brother, who (to my dismay) had nothing to share but another dreaded tract. His read, *Why Christians Should Observe Christmas*. I went home that night frustrated, my mind reeling.

The next day after Sunday assembly, I was standing in the stairwell that led up to the church foyer, when I felt one of the brothers brush past me on his way up the stairs. He glanced momentarily to acknowledge my presence, smiled, and asked nonchalantly "Got your tree up yet?" I paused for a moment and then coyly replied, "Well... I don't celebrate Christmas." Without much thought, the brother quickly retorted, "You don't celebrate Christmas? What's the matter with you?" I immediately blushed, realizing that everybody in the stairwell had heard our exchange. Had I sinned in some way? I began to wonder what I had gotten myself into.

Completely exasperated and heartbroken, I spent Christmas 200 miles north, alone in a hotel room, because I didn't want to offend anyone.

I tell this story to make a critical point—most new Christians are not equipped with enough biblical knowledge to make sense of conflicting viewpoints. I was a 25-year-old babe in Christ with very little spiritual foundation, and the misplaced words of a select few sent me on a downward spiral. I truly believe that my negative experience could have been avoided had the brothers taken the time to think about the needs of a new Christian and the safety of his soul. That's what being a brother's keeper is really all about.

GOD'S FAMILY

Mark 10:28-30 paints a wonderful picture of the Christian family. When one becomes a Christian, his family increases a hundredfold! While it's easy to focus on this as an incredible gift, we must also consider the responsibility this places on the older Christian. Not only do we receive family when we're baptized into Christ, but we become the family Jesus promised to other Christians. By treating the new brother or sister as family, we fulfill one of the most powerful promises our Savior ever made. The church is

God's family, so consider how important it is to Him. He sent His Son to die a cruel death for it.

Think for a moment about your congregation over the last few years. Have some brethren given in to Satan's powerful influence and returned to the world? Ask yourself a few questions:

- Do I care that they left?
- Did I try to stop them from leaving, or have I tried to bring them back?
- Who's taken the time to regularly study and socialize with them, proving they are family?
- What could I do differently from this day forward to make sure that souls are safe in the church?
- Would a concerted brother's keeper ministry engage new Christians to the point that they would not fall away?

Sadly and inevitably, some Christians will lose focus and slip back into the world. Demas, a man who personally worked with the apostle Paul, loved the present world too much and left the church (2 Timothy 4:10). There are certainly those today who stumble into the same snare. We must be careful not to label those who fall away as "bad soil" and ignore our responsibility to them. Instead, we must attempt to prevent their departure by setting a good example and showing genuine care and concern for them.

We must also work to develop relationships that extend

beyond the confines of the church foyer. A firm handshake or pat on the back before Sunday service is nice and can be encouraging, but should that be the sum total of our relationship to one another? Imagine if you treated your parents or grandparents in like manner. God expects more of His children.

The community of people that comprised the New Testament church we read of in Acts was so close-knit that many sold their possessions and property to care for one another. Consider also the example of the apostle Paul, who spent just weeks with the church in Thessalonica, yet could not bear to be kept in the dark about their condition (1 Thessalonians 3:5). We should exhibit the same attitude of concern toward our brothers and sisters today!

If you are a mature saint, treat the new Christian like you would a grandchild. If you are the same age, treat him like a sibling. We must move beyond pleasantries and engage each other like we would our own blood relatives.

THE MOTIVATION OF A BROTHER'S KEEPER

Have you ever seen a dog eat its own vomit? Undoubtedly, the very thought makes you cringe. In 2 Peter 2:20-22, the Holy Spirit uses this analogy to illustrate the end horror of anyone who leaves the Lord to return to worldly living. In verse 21, the Scripture says, "it would have been better to never have known the way of righteousness." God admonishes us not only to personally remain faithful, but also to love our brothers in such a way that they don't face this either. The eternal safety of the soul is the key motivator to becoming a better brother's keeper.

THE MINDSET OF A BROTHER'S KEEPER

Have you read Romans 14 lately? If not, I would encourage you to read it in its entirety before continuing on. This chapter, which serves as God's handbook on how to treat the new babe in Christ, makes it clear that while new Christians may be zealous, thankful, excited, and evangelistic, they are ultimately weak, lacking in spiritual wisdom, and in need of guidance from mature brethren. Always make sure they are welcomed for who they are—joint heirs with Jesus—and focus on their needs. New Christians will trust you to make them more like Jesus and will lean on your faith and experience as a crutch for some time.

Do you remember what it was like to be a new Christian, recently snatched from the world and its pleasures? Committing to Jesus often requires a very drastic lifestyle change, one in which old behaviors, habits, friends, and places must be changed. Understanding the mindset of the babe and empathizing with them as they grow is key to successfully keeping them "safe in the fold."

THE NEW CHRISTIAN IS...

You may find it hard to remember exactly what it was like

to be a new Christian. Don't underestimate the benefit of walking a mile in their shoes. You will gain valuable insight to help you identify with them in a genuine way. In this process of learning to relate, let's look at some qualities of the typical new Christian.

Struggling

In the parable of the sower, there are those who "have no root in themselves, but endure for a while; then, when tribulation or persecution arises on account of the word, immediately they fall away" (Mark 4:17). Christians in all phases of their walk struggle with sin, but the new babe is likely attempting to alter deeply ingrained behaviors, values, morals and habits. We must immediately provide the opportunity for new Christians to develop roots in order to help them defend against Satan's attacks.

Cautious

Be sure to listen to new Christians very carefully. Most will be hesitant to share deep concerns and struggles until they get to know you very well. It may take weeks or months and probably won't happen until they truly believe that you care. Be patient. They are sorting out many issues, which they will probably reveal in time.

Thirsty for Truth

The new Christian is thirsty for spiritual truth. He has made a huge lifestyle change and wants to equip himself with knowledge to support his changed behavior and evangelistic efforts. Just remember to feed the new Christian "milk" because it is all he can handle. He may physically be a 40-year-old man, but spiritually, he is an infant. Respect him as a man, but care for his spiritual needs with kindness and gentleness, as a mother with her baby.

Evangelistic

New Christians tend to be very evangelistic and want to smother their friends and family with the good news they've found, but typically have incomplete answers and an unrefined approach. We must channel their excitement so that they do not drive their family and friends away, but draw them to Jesus.

Just be careful not to douse their excitement for the Lord! Gently caution them, calling to mind the example of Jesus. There is a thought I mention to new Christians often: "You made the life change. Your friends and family did not. Be careful."

Transitioning

The new Christian's everyday life has been dramatically transformed. Their friends and family members probably treat them differently and may resort to ridicule or persecution. Mature Christians must be ready to help new converts while their young faith is being tested. Generally, it takes a year or so of consistent one-on-one study to bring a new Christian to the point where they're able to stand on their own faith. For some, it takes longer. Living like Jesus is no small undertaking, and it's foolish to expect the babe in Christ to reach maturity instantaneously.

Sensitive

Most mature Christians have developed relationships with one another that allow them to speak matter-of-factly without fear of offense. The new Christian, on the other hand, is more sensitive to criticism, even if presented in a constructive manner. We must get to know them and help them build relationships so that they're comfortable receiving advice, admonition, and even rebuke (when necessary).

Family

In Genesis, we see our amazing God create a universe beyond understanding, all so that man could inhabit the earth (Isaiah 45:18). God immediately established the framework by which man would populate the earth by marrying Adam and Eve. They would bear children who would eventually leave home to begin new families.

The family unit has been so butchered and misconstrued by human thinking that we lose the Godly concept of family all too often. When the local church understands itself to be God's family and operates accordingly, the new Christian is taken aback by the genuine love and concern they see and feel.

THE NEW CHRISTIAN NEEDS...

Genuine Acceptance

The new Christian needs to be shown unconditional love, in spite of his habitual sins, poor hygiene, disabilities, or any other condition that makes us uncomfortable. Some need a little more work than others, and that's fine. Jesus didn't die for the beautiful, but for sinners: "God chose what is foolish in the world to shame the wise; God chose what is weak in the world to shame the strong" (1 Corinthians 1:27).

Relationships

Introduce the new Christian to someone who has gone through a similar life experience or has a compatible personality as soon as possible. Familiarity with others gives strength and comfort to the new babe, which aids in the process of assimilation. Always remember Christ's plea for unity and strive to find the ways in which we can come together as family.

Encouragement

Our encouragement must be genuine, not sugar-coated. Sincere praise for the choice they have made to follow Jesus and the follow-up with them is so necessary. Something as simple as asking the new Christian to sit with you during worship can provide a huge morale boost. It screams, "I accept you and want to be with you!" Think about how encouraging it is to feel important.

Realistic Expectations for Growth

The new Christian has a great desire to please you because they appreciate the time you are spending with them. Help them find ways to participate or minister to others, but be very careful not to require too much too soon. Look for specific traits or abilities like a good memory, an aptitude to teach, or gentleness with others, and try to help them hone their skills to serve and spread the gospel. It can also be beneficial to help them with seemingly insignificant matters, like memorizing the books of the Bible in sequence. Sometimes these "little wins" can go a long way for the new Christian.

Resources

Ask the apostle Paul about "zeal without knowledge"—it can be quite destructive! There are so many great resources to help the new Christian answer difficult questions and prepare to engage others in spiritual conversation, but most don't know where to start looking. You can help them find people and resources in your congregation (church library, small group meetings, weekly Bible studies, etc.) or point them to the internet for high-quality material. We highly recommend the following sites, which are all maintained by members of the Lord's church: apologeticspress.org, focuspress.org and wvbs.org.

THE NEW CHRISTIAN PROVIDES...

Opportunity for the Flock

A whirlwind of activity is generated when a few new Christians are added to the local flock! They often bring skills, personalities, and networks that were completely missing from the picture before. Young Christians energize the old, and mature Christians provide wisdom to the babes. Meanwhile, the congregation that does not evangelize stagnates and dies.

Unspeakable Joy

Picture yourself opening up your home to a young couple that has recently put the Lord on in baptism. After time, the young man you've befriended agrees to lead prayer in the assembly. His voice cracks and he stumbles over his words, yet you have tears of joy running down your cheeks because God has allowed you to be a part of this young man's spiritual development. You know where he once was and where he will end up if he continues to allow God to guide him. This is one addiction that you don't need to treat. You'll keep wanting more and more, and that's precisely the way God wants us to feel.

Valuable Feedback

When one of our study groups has progressed for a few months, and the new Christian has a good understanding of the "bring, teach, keep" methodology, I always ask for the students' thoughts and suggestions. Their verbal answers and body language either reinforce what I'm doing or expose the holes in my method—both of which help me make refinements for future groups. As you evangelize lost souls, solicit their feedback to improve your approach.

CREATING THE OPTIMUM ENVIRONMENT

I try to conduct most of the brother's keeper groups I lead in somebody's home because I believe that the informal environment of a home is the perfect setting for the new Christian to study and socialize with others. The first century church met in homes for a number of reasons (to be free from persecution, to regularly study and share meals, they didn't own a church building, etc.), and I think we would do well to follow their example. Let me share some thoughts and suggestions based on how I typically run a home study group. Please take these ideas and either adjust or build upon them to best suit your group and the new Christians that join you.

At the beginning of the study period, have one of the members say a prayer, then ask the new Christian if there are any questions on his mind—this is a must! The new Christian may be struggling with a number of issues and you want to address those issues first and foremost. On many occasions, you will never even get to the study agenda because the new Christian has so many pressing concerns. Remember, these studies are all about him or her. As a brother's keeper, you want to make sure they are equipped to battle against Satan's influence.

FOOD *for* THOUGHT

Some hosting members choose to serve food before or after the study. The fellowship can be great, but should be kept separate from the scheduled study time for two reasons: (1) You want to make the process easy to duplicate and don't want food preparation to stop someone from hosting a study. (2) Stopping to chew a mouth full of roast beef or crunching incessantly on a cracker will bring the discussion to a screeching halt. On the other hand, a sip of coffee, tea or water will not hinder discussion and is appropriate during the study period.

At some point, the new Christian will probably ask a question that is either counter productive to or inappropriate for a beginner study. If you're meeting for the first or second study and your new brother asks you to explain the numerology in Revelation, kindly steer him in a different direction. Tell him it's a great question and write it down for later, explaining that there's a great deal of foundational material that needs to be understood before you can cover such a deep topic.

If there are no questions, start the session with a short lesson, presented orally or in video format. One of my favorite video series is Convicted by Brad Harrub. Brad uses many evidences to prove that the Bible is from God, while refuting popular false doctrines such as evolution and the Big Bang theory. Apologetics really whet the new Christian's appetite for more, as they see so many wonderful truths revealed that they had never been taught (I had one young lady get angry because of the blatant lies she was being taught in her high school classes)! There are volumes of excellent media choices to use, so do some investigation to find one that works best for you and your environment.

If using a video, break the lesson into 30 minute segments, and then discuss the topic at hand for an hour or so. If presenting the lesson orally, make sure there is regular interaction between you and the new Christian. Avoid lecturing—it has been proven that the adult mind can only focus for about 8 minutes at a time without changing gears! Pose a question, introduce a graphic, or share an anecdote to break up the material.

Upon completion of the series of prepared lessons or videos, ask what areas of study the new Christian would like to explore. Continue to work with them until they can stand firm on their own faith. Your ultimate goal is to build a foundation that will serve the new Christians for the rest of their lives and to equip them with enough evidence to defend their beliefs when questioned.

FOOD *for* THOUGHT

Remember to always ask God for wisdom and don't be afraid to pull in a more knowledgeable or experienced teacher, if necessary. Evangelism is not a one man show, but a family affair!

This basic framework has been very successful for me as I've studied with numerous new brothers and sisters. However, it is far from all-inclusive. Customize it to fit the needs of the new Christians you invite to your home study.

MEETING THEIR SOCIAL NEEDS

The Lord has a place in the church for every willing person on this earth. But make no mistake—it takes a lot of time and effort on the part of Christians to keep souls faithful. That is why it is so necessary for us to socialize the new Christian with as many brethren as possible apart from a Bible study setting or worship assembly. We need to reinforce that they are literally part of the family of God by treating them like family throughout the entire week. What would your home life be like if you only socialized with your spouse and children once or twice a week? Quite shallow, indeed. We have to seek deeper relationships with Christians, both new and old.

FOOD *for* THOUGHT

Does your congregation have a "socialization system" in place for new Christians? Try this:

Start by asking 4 families to invite the new Christian over for dinner, one a week over the span of a month. The "host" family should invite a few other families from the congregation. Make it informal and fun with dinner, games and casual conversation. After the first week, the second family will invite the new Christian to their place for dinner along with a few different families.

You can see that each night the new Christian meets 7-10 new people, and over the course of a month has been introduced to dozens! The setting is relaxed and non-threatening, and the systematic approach places the new Christian into many homes with many people. He will have to feel like a part of what he reads about in the New Testament church!

Too Much Socialization?

I have counseled many new Christians to be careful about the amount of time they spend away from their non-Christian spouses and families at Bible studies, assemblies, and informal gatherings. They must not create a sense of neglect or abandonment if they wish to lead their loved ones to the Savior. Being pulled in two directions is difficult, but they must balance their home life and church activity with the utmost care and concern.

Worshipping God on the first day of the week in the assembly of the saints is not optional, as it's an example we see clearly in the New Testament. However, the mid-week class is our addition that we must not bind on the new Christian, especially if it hurts the chance of a spouse being drawn to the Savior. If coming to both a home study and the mid-week congregational Bible class would hurt the relationship between the new Christian and his or her spouse, then they should give up the mid-week study and go to the home group where personal attention is given.

WANT TO BE A BROTHER'S KEEPER?

At this point, it should be clear why I chose to present the role of the brother's keeper first. A strong brother's keeper effort both prepares a congregation for growth and helps new babes become strong Christians. Should you determine to step up and become a brother's keeper, you will be a tremendous force in evangelism. Many find that when they get their feet wet in this role, they also develop talent as bringers and teachers. Determine what your God-given ability is now, strive to become better at it, and see where He leads you. "Bloom where you're planted" is a common piece of advice in which I see great wisdom!

Bringers

Fear of rejection has doused the evangelistic fire of so many Christians, yet "bringing" is a task that's a whole lot easier than Satan wants us to believe. He's made us believe that if we offer Jesus to people and they say no, we have failed and should give up. Let me reassure you that success or failure in evangelism is not based on the response of the hearer. If we offer Jesus to people and they answer "no," we are still a resounding success in the eyes of God because we have offered the gospel.

Everything we do must begin with prayer for understanding and wisdom to follow through with the mission of the church. I believe that we need to ask God to bring seekers into our lives on a daily basis. "Seek and ye shall find" is not just a catchy phrase for our children to sing about, but a promise from God, which he is sure to follow through with if we ask in faith (Matthew 7:7).

THREE BEINGS INVOLVED IN BRINGING

There are at least three parties involved every time an attempt is made to bring a soul to Christ: God, me, and the hearer. Mentally draw a thick line between each of those entities, a "caution strip" of sorts. Each line represents a separation of responsibility and accountability that we cannot cross when trying to bring the lost to Jesus Christ.

1. God

I begin with God because there is little to explain. He perfectly fulfills His role in evangelism without fail. Think about these characteristics of God and how they inform our evangelistic efforts:

- God is not a respecter of persons (Acts 10:34).
- God never misses a seeking soul (Psalm 121:3-4).
- God wants all men to be saved (1 Timothy 2:4).
- God grants the increase (1 Corinthians 3:7).

He does all of the hard work, and He's given us His Word as a guide to boot! When we think about His promises and His all-powerful ability, it gives us a limitless measure of confidence to reach out to the lost.

However, we must always be careful not to inadvertently assume the responsibility of God when trying to evangelize. Often, when an individual refuses to hear the gospel, we feel that we have failed, as if there were something more powerful, eloquent, or moving that we could have said or done. The inherent problem with this kind of thinking is that we forget who grants increase. If a person is truly seeking, and we kindly offer them the opportunity to study or worship, they will make the effort to learn more. If they are not seeking, we must accept their "no" and move on to another person without feeling guilty.

FOOD *for* THOUGHT

There's a very good reason why granting increase is always in God's hands and never in ours—think about the partiality of man! We tend to hold back increase from those we don't care for and grant extra increase to our loved ones.

Think about the anecdote that James shares in the second chapter of his letter: "My brothers, show no partiality as you hold the faith in our Lord Jesus Christ, the Lord of glory. For if a man wearing a gold ring and fine clothing comes into your assembly, and a poor man in shabby clothing also comes in, and if you pay attention to the one who wears the fine clothing and say, "You sit here in a good place," while you say to the poor man, "You stand over there," or, "Sit down at my feet," have you not then made distinctions among yourselves and become judges with evil thoughts?" (James 2:2). Mankind doesn't exactly have a pristine record when it comes to fairness!

Consider the example of Jesus in Matthew 19:16-30. When the rich young ruler asked Jesus what he must do to inherit eternal life, the Master told him, "Go sell what you have, give it to the poor, and follow me." The young ruler walked away sorrowful because he had many possessions. We tend to focus on the plight of the young ruler, but think about Jesus' response to the young ruler? Did he chase after the young man to negotiate the terms of salvation? Did he try to get him to stop and realize that he was the Messiah?" He did neither. Instead, Jesus allowed the young man to walk away. Although it seems like the young man might have been seeking, his ultimate refusal shows that he wasn't ready to commit to Jesus.

As you bring, always remember that the Master Himself allowed someone to walk away. It would behoove us to do likewise. The power of the gospel does not depend on how we present it, so long as we speak with kindness and humility. The power is in the Word, which God promises will transform those who diligently seek Him.

2. Me

At a seminar in Arkansas, I asked a young teen if he wanted something for which he would have to get money from his parents. He responded emphatically, "Yes, I need a new cell phone." I then inquired if he would approach his dad for the new phone after hearing his parents discussing their financial woes. Without hesitation, he responded, "No, the odds are small that I'd get it."

From a very early age, we learn to size up situations in order to determine a course of action toward a desired result. Evangelism works the same way. To achieve our desired result (the opportunity to share the gospel), we must recognize that each situation requires a different approach. There's a time to speak, a time to listen, a time to stay silent, and a time to boldly proclaim the truth. The spectrum of Jesus' actions ranges from tenderly placing a child on His lap to kicking over tables in the temple area. Certainly, He understood that every situation demands a different response to accomplish the desired result. Likewise, God has given us the intellect and experience needed to weed out the effective methods from the ineffective.

Imagine knocking on a door in your neighborhood. When the resident opens the door, you begin to preach a fire and brimstone message—"If you aren't immersed into Christ you will go to hell when you die! Can you say no to Jesus?!" The resident slams the door in your face. Unshaken, you continue through the neighborhood from house to house, proclaiming the same message and receiving the same response. Would it be fair to say that there are quite a few adjustments that need to be made to your approach?

It is not arrogant to analyze the abilities God has blessed you with if the end goal is to improve your effectiveness in evangelism. In fact, He wants us to do this! Get out a piece of paper and write down your known abilities, things like "good sense of humor," "kind," "enduring patience," and so on. Search yourself and write down any positive talent or trait that could be an asset to others. Then, should you decide to, join with your spouse or a close brother or sister to help complete the list. We don't always see (or choose to see) the gifts we possess, and others may help us create a more complete picture. Seeing abstract concepts in print can really help you take note of and understand the "tools" God has given you. And keep in mind that this list is only the beginning! In Ephesians 3:20, Paul writes that God can do "exceeding abundantly above what we ask or think according to the power that works within us." As you develop in evangelism, God will grant continued growth beyond your current level of skill!

Breaking the Ice

Learning how to properly approach a potential seeker can be daunting at first, but after time almost becomes second nature. I've affectionately dubbed one of my preferred methods "fishing." When in a conversation with a stranger or acquaintance, I throw out a few "worms" (subtle references or questions) to hopefully spark interest.

A few years ago, the company I worked for was contracted to take care of the snow removal around a senior care facility. One day, while I was shoveling sidewalks, a resident whom I had never met came out and thanked me for the care my company showed. Our conversation went something like this:

Resident: "How much longer will it be 'til you're finished?"

Chuck: "Well, it looks like we've done all we can do. I'll let the salt and the Good Lord's sunshine finish this job."

Resident: "You really go way out of the way to do more than you have to."

Chuck: "The Lord sees everything, and I believe He would want me to do what I can, even if it means we stay out here a bit more to make sure it's safe for the residents."

With this he went silent and slowly walked away. The look on his face told me that he wasn't seeking. Knowing that I would see him many more times (we also took care of the property in the summer), I just let him walk away. We would have conversations in the future, and I would again go "fishing" with him then. The seed had been planted.

Keep in mind that a "no" answer does not denote absolute failure. Do not let Satan convince you of that lie! By planting a seed of thought, you achieve a tremendous victory in the sight of God because you put yourself in the position to give someone a chance to know Jesus. I have found that "no" often means "not now." It happens so often—a person will come back after weeks, months, or years to see if you're still involved with the church. This is their way of saying "I now am seeking and I remembered your example."

In 2010, I finished a 10 week study with a man, and then did not see him for six months. He came back to the church building asking to meet again and, shortly thereafter, decided to become a Christian. All that time, he was "counting the cost" of following Jesus. What good would it have done for me to wallow in self-pity, searching for where I failed and dwelling on what I could have said while this man was absent? We must remember that God grants the increase and continue to press forward, even when it seems that our efforts have been in vain.

How to Determine if Someone is Seeking

I'm often asked how to determine if someone is seeking. As bringers, we must master the ability to gauge others' interest in the gospel. It is possible to offer too little, and it is possible to overwhelm and push people away. A little bit of genuineness, kindness and courage goes a long way.

As you endeavor to find seekers, try to connect with people on a practical level, whether it be holding the door for an elderly lady in the midst of a snowstorm or bagging your own groceries in the checkout lane. Do something even slightly "out of the ordinary" and others will surely take notice. Then, when you have their attention, inject snippets of your daily walk with the Lord into your conversation. A true seeker will latch on to these tidbits. If they show no interest (or change the subject!), you'll know they are not currently seeking. Kindly go your way, knowing that your gracious speech and faithful example have planted a seed that may sprout and bloom at a later time.

We can be sure this strategy works because the Savior

Himself modeled it for us! Consider His conversation with the Samaritan woman at Jacob's Well in John 4. Jesus began his approach with a practical request by simply asking the woman for water. He could have drawn the water Himself, but knew that would not impact the woman. Being a Jew, the mere fact that he conversed with a Samaritan woman was extremely extraordinary.

Upon securing the woman's attention, Jesus guided the conversation to her salvation needs. She was so moved that she immediately ran home to tell the townspeople about her conversation with Jesus, and they returned to Him in droves, confessing Him as the "Savior of the world" (John 4:42). Like the Savior, take full advantage of your interactions with others because there is potential for us to reach out with the gospel in almost any situation.

I remember, not long ago, sitting in the hospital with a sister while her husband underwent surgery. After the procedure was successfully completed, I made my way to the second-floor lobby to head home for the day. As I approached the elevator, I immediately took note of a rather jovial man coming from the opposite side of the lobby. We both entered the elevator and I asked if he was going down. "Yes," he said with a smile. "Great," I responded, "I'll follow you down. I've spent so many hours walking these halls that people are calling me doctor!"

The man laughed and asked me if I was visiting family. "No," I told him, "I'm from the Waterford church of Christ and was sitting with a brother's wife while he was in surgery." He asked if my friend was fine (which I thought was very kind) then, to my excitement, inquired, "And what church did you say you are from?" I gave him my business card with a small map to the building and told him he would be an honored guest at any of our services. The elevator stopped, the door opened, and we both stepped into the first floor lobby. "I will look you up!" he exclaimed with a smile, and we parted ways.

You may find this situation similar to the story of Brock, though the outcome was notably different. Instead of trying to explain doctrine or quote scripture, I used the opportunity to see if the man was currently seeking and to lay a foundation for the future.

Just a few weeks later, he called me to follow up on my offer to worship. The seed I planted fell on fertile soil, and God granted increase according to His will.

Respond, Don't React

When others respond to our evangelistic attempts with courtesy, it's quite easy to leave the door open for future engagement, even if they initially decline. Think again about my encounter in the hospital elevator, but imagine that the man had kindly refused to accept my business card, stating that he had no interest in attending a worship service. I believe it would have been appropriate to simply say, "The offer is always open should you change your mind."

Unfortunately, our attempts to evangelize are not always received so amiably. Suppose instead that the man had responded harshly, shouting "You Bible thumpers walk around like you're perfect. I hate it when people like you try to cram the Bible down my throat." In a situation like this, it's much harder to respond in a Christ-like manner. Our human instincts cause us to perceive confrontation as danger and react in defense.

Resist the urge to fight back at all costs! Instead, respond with grace and empathy: "I don't blame you for hating it. I do too. You know, I have a friend who does a timeline of the Bible that really helped me understand it all better. I just thought you might be interested." Leave them remembering how kindly you treated them after being verbally assailed.

Some people will be offended no matter how they are approached, though our critical and judgmental methods are typically the cause of such scathing reactions. Should we expect to smack the bee hive and not get stung? A wise brother once preached that we need to "leave our crowbars at home." In other words, we must let God open doors for us instead of trying force open those that he has not unlocked.

3. The Hearer

If you were not raised in the church, stop and think about your life before you became a Christian. I dare say the majority of us thought we were pretty good people and had a chance to make it to Heaven when we died. The truth, of course, is that not one soul has even the remotest chance of reaching Heaven outside of Jesus (John 14:6). Our own wisdom led us to that false conclusion.

We must remember that it is not flesh and blood that we're battling against (Ephesians 6:12). Our battle is against the powers of darkness that influence the thinking of lost souls. Since we do not possess the power to defeat that thinking (the gospel is God's power unto salvation, Romans 1:16), our responsibility is to do everything we can to make the environment rich for the lost soul to allow us the opportunity to teach him.

There is no pre-written script or catchy phrase that will convict a hearer. Instead, it is a kind demeanor and genuine care that makes an indelible impact. We need to develop the ability to hear them when they say "no." This is not a sales call where you push until they say no seven times before you listen. Say something gentle and kind like, "If you ever change your mind, let me know," and let it go.

It's amazing to think about human reasoning in comparison to God's infinite wisdom. We do not allow our children to determine their own bedtime, the amount of allowance they will receive, or the chores they must complete. Neither does a prospective employee tell the owner of a company the wage he will receive or the benefits he'll enjoy. Yet, for some reason, people expect their relationship with God to be different. So many tell God how they will worship and how they will be saved. How can they expect God to accept this? The world has succumb to Satan, and we must be aware of its effect on the hearer.

Teachers

Fully understanding the impact of the Gospel on a seeker's heart is one of the great challenges of teaching the lost. A good friend of mine once said that "if we try to draw people with a slick presentation, we have to keep them with slick presentations. If we try to draw them with a positive promise, then we have to keep them with positive promises. There is still only one thing that makes Christians, period, and that's the Gospel. When we draw them with the Gospel, it is the Gospel that will maintain them. If they have no interest in the Gospel, we have nothing else to offer and they must be allowed to walk away."

I continue to use the Bible timeline, a chronological overview of the Bible, as my preferred teaching method for a number of reasons, the foremost being that it is 100% gospel-focused. Every event in the Bible points either forward or back to the Savior, and the timeline highlights the interconnectedness of the Bible beautifully. With seekers and new Christians, I typically start by presenting a number of Christian evidences from the book of Genesis. Apologetics help the seeker understand that the Bible is from God, develop an awe of what God has revealed, and build a strong foundation as they're being led to Christ. This is a tremendously non-threatening way to pique interest and elicit critical thinking.

I spend a lot of time walking through the Old Testament, showing through fulfilled prophecy that Jesus was the only possible individual who met the requirements to be our Savior. It is imperative that seekers are converted to Jesus, not baptism, the Bible, or the church of Christ. The Old Testament is also chock full of information that, when honestly considered, completely destroys the popular notion that the Bible is a book of fairy tales or fables. Weaving secular history into the biblical narrative further validates the accuracy and credibility of the Bible in the mind of the hearer.

Practically speaking, the timeline is successful because it respects the hearer. It is a teaching method that can be easily tailored to the individual's current knowledge and understanding of the Bible and is adaptable to all ages. You can move rapidly through, even skip parts, choosing what you believe is necessary for the hearer to know to get them to Jesus. Because each week's lesson builds upon what was taught the previous week, the seeker is not bombarded with advanced material from the outset. Rather, they are taught as they are able to bear (Mark 4:33). The comfortable pace and gradual release of information gives the listener time to count the cost of discipleship while they are increasing their faith and knowledge.

Lastly, the timeline has been so effective for me because it's just downright interesting. It's not uncommon for seekers to bring their friends and family along after sitting through only one session. On many occasions, I've taught the first lesson two or three times consecutively to accommodate those brought along by the original student! Trust me on this one: the magic is not in the delivery, but in the words and thoughts of our almighty God. Present the gospel unadulterated, and true seekers will express interest.

CONDUCTING A TIMELINE PRESENTATION

Let me describe some ground rules for a typical study session to give you a better understanding of the manner in which I study with seekers. Whether you use the timeline or your own teaching method, the following suggestions will prove beneficial.

The leader must lead the study.

In a small group setting, it's extremely important that the leader come across as the "professor," so that the students will have confidence in what he is saying, though it's certainly not necessary to answer every question right away or add deep insights. The leader should not inject every bit of knowledge he possesses about Creation, Abraham, Moses, David or any other topic into the presentation. The overarching goal is to get the seeker to see Jesus as the Son of God and Savior of the world through the fulfillment of the Old Testament prophecies. We live in a biblically illiterate world, so take it at their pace, no matter how slow or shallow that may seem to the mature Christians in your group.

Do not dispute doctrine in front of your students.

Make sure there are no disputes between Christians in the midst of the study period. Should two members disagree on a point of doctrine (indwelling of the Holy Spirit, for instance), it can and should be discussed at length in another setting. However, the primary focus of the study is the seeker. You must make the environment as rich as possible for them to receive Jesus.

Entertain questions at the beginning of the study.

Your students will probably be full of questions as they learn about the Bible. As they bring their inquiries to you, let them know that you'll answer in one of three ways:

- By using Scripture as evidence of a belief.
- By giving an opinion on the matter with an added caution that you are not certain and more study may be needed.
- By assuring them that the question is good and will be covered later in the timeline presentation. Have them write it down so they do not forget, and continue leading them through the Bible toward Christ. You don't want to talk about New Testament doctrine until they are convinced that Jesus is the Messiah.

Don't let the seeker feel like a kindergartner in college.

So often, a group leader will purposely omit material from a study because he is gauging the student's reaction to what is being taught and adjusting the depth of the conversation. If other Christians at the study constantly add tangential insight and information, the lost soul will begin to feel like a grade school student in a Ph.D. program. Remember, relationship building is the primary role of mature Christians who attend a study with a seeker. I like to call them my "grinners" because encouragement is their primary role.

Read the students' reactions.

Watch their body language to gauge which topics may be "hot button" issues or great points of interest. It may also help you determine whether you're going too slow or too fast. This is one of the great benefits of studying with a group—often, the leader is so engrossed with the material that he is not able to pick up on body language, whereas the "grinners" in the group can.

Stick around afterward and get to know the students.

Mature Christians can at times take the brotherhood for granted because we forget how fantastic it was when we got our first taste. Make sure to incorporate time for fellowship in your study group. By showing genuine interest, you open up a whole new world of friendship to your students.

I have found that the timeline presentation is a tremendous training tool to help all members develop their evangelistic gifts. It is a non-confrontational method that can be used to help Christians become confident teachers. It gives bringers an easy way to invite their friends and family to study the Word in a comfortable environment. And, it provides fertile ground for the brother's keepers to utilize their wonderful talents. This model is effective because it follows the wisdom that is from above (James 3:17).

Conclusion

A few years ago, at an evangelism seminar in Arkansas, I had the good fortune of meeting a young woman named Joni. One night after my presentation, she approached me distraught because she really wanted to reach out to people but wasn't comfortable with her ability to teach. I reassured her that God could help her become a powerful force in evangelism and shared with her the full picture of the biblical model of evangelism. She was elated that she could fulfill her role as a bringer and not have to teach. The next Thursday, Joni invited her supervisor to Bible class. Although her supervisor didn't come, Joni was excited to finally see her place in evangelism. And she was a success in the eyes of God because she offered a lost soul a chance to hear the Gospel!

Another sister in her 70s told me that she couldn't see herself functioning as a bringer, teacher or brother's keeper. I challenged her to open her home up to about 5 or 6 people for a Bible study, making sure she understood that she wouldn't have to cook, teach, or even clean her house beforehand. All she would have to do is let the brethren use her home to welcome and teach a new Christian. A huge smile spread across her face as she ran the idea through her mind, and the rest, as they say, is history. The dear sister finally discovered her role in evangelism, when weeks earlier she completely doubted her ability to serve in any capacity.

I gave a preview copy of this book to a young man in our congregation who had recently become a Christian. Weeks later, he called me on the phone with great excitement in his voice. "Chuck," he said, "I finally understand where I fit into the model of evangelism!" I beamed, fully expecting him to tell me that he saw himself as a bringer, teacher or brother's keeper. Instead he told me, so enthusiastically, "I'm a brother who needs to be kept!" As tears welled up in my eyes, he went on to tell me that he had so many questions that we wanted to know the answers to in order to share his faith with his family and friends. It had never occurred to me that someone would read this material and come to that conclusion!

It's stories like these that affirm my faith in the biblical model of evangelism time and time again. When we fully understand and embrace the God-designed method of bringing souls into contact with Jesus and keeping them safe in the flock, there are no limits to the change God can affect through His church. Truly, the "eye has not seen nor ear heard, neither have entered into the heart of man, what the Lord has in store for those who love Him" (1 Corinthians 2:9). If we believe and act accordingly, God "is able to do exceeding abundantly above what we ask or think, according to the power that works within us" (Ephesians

3:20). I sincerely hope that this book has inspired you to take a fresh look at your role in evangelism. May the Lord bless your endeavors to serve Him faithfully.

From the Authors

Firstly, my thankfulness to God must be noted. We Christians are incredibly blessed to be a part of His kingdom, standing cleansed in Jesus. Secondly, I thank my wife Michelle. The thousands of hours that we have spent together, sharing thoughts and insights have been invaluable. Without her support, there's no way that you would be holding this book in your hands. Michelle, I love you and am very grateful. Lastly, I want to thank the brethren that have influenced me and those that have added tremendous input to this material. To begin to name them all would be an impossible task. However, there are two couples that I must acknowledge specifically: Eric and Cindy Richardson and Paul and Bev Schandevel.

Eric and Cindy Richardson have supported Michelle and I in so many ways and it's with heartfelt gratitude that I simply say "thank you for everything you've done."

Paul was a co-worker of mine at a Hilton hotel 30 years ago, and he and his wife Bev were amazing examples of Jesus to me. I was not seeking salvation at the time, but Paul would still invite me to worship, Bible study, and various church functions. We were friends for a period of two years, when finally, as he was leaving Michigan to further his career, I stopped him and asked, "What is it about you that makes you so different?" His response was simple, yet so profound: "Chuck, when you die there are two books opened, the book of your life and the Bible. If they don't match, you don't make it." His words have stuck with me all of these years, and I still stay in close contact with Paul and Bev. We may go six months without speaking, but when we do it's as if we'd been talking daily. God has blessed my life so much through Paul and Bev!

~ Chuck Anderson

Thank you to my beautiful wife Bethany, my spunky daughter Penelope, my friend and co-author Chuck Anderson, my awesome church family at Waterford, and last—but certainly not least—my Lord and Savior, Jesus Christ. All glory, honor and praise belongs to Him. Without His grace and mercy, we would be irrevocably lost. I hope that this book is a reflection of his love and a blessing to those who seek to grow in evangelism.

~ John Furness

Made in the USA
Monee, IL
19 October 2023

44796860R00046